My Favorite Horses

Morgan Horses Are My Favorite!

Elaine Landau

LERNER PUBLICATIONS COMPANY • MINNEAPOLIS

Lerner Publications Company
A division of Lerner Publishing Group, Inc.
241 First Avenue North
Minneapolis, MN 55401 U.S.A.

Website address: www.lernerbooks.com

Library of Congress Cataloging-in-Publication Data

Landau, Elaine.
    Morgan horses are my favorite! / by Elaine Landau.
        p.   cm. — (My favorite horses)
    Includes index.
    ISBN 978-0-7613-6536-5 (lib. bdg. : alk. paper)
    1. Morgan horse—Juvenile literature. I. Title.
  SF293.M8L36 2012
    636.1'77—dc22   2011011665

Manufactured in the United States of America
1 — PP — 12/31/11

PHOTO ACKNOWLEDGEMENTS

The images in this book are used with the permission of: backgrounds © iStockphoto.com/nolimitpictures; © B. Speckart/Shutterstock Images, p. 1; © Barbara O'Brien Photography pp. 4, 7, 16, 22; © Tierfotoagentur/R.Richter/Alamy, p. 6; © Darlene Wohlart, pp. 8, 9, 10-11, 15, 17, 18, 19, 20, 21; © Andre Jenny/Alamy, p. 12; © Peter Newark American Pictures/The Bridgeman Art Library, p. 13; © MPI/Stringer/ Archive Photos/Getty Images, p. 14.

Front Cover and Back Cover: © Barbara O'Brien Photography.

Main body text set in Atelier Sans ITC Std 16/24.
Typeface provided by International Typeface Corp.

TABLE OF CONTENTS

INTRODUCTION
YOUR DREAM HORSE

What's your dream horse?

Is it a handsome animal that's fast and strong? Would your dream horse also be smart and loyal? If so, you could easily fall for the Morgan horse. It's one of the best-liked horses in the country.

A Morgan horse may sound perfect for you, but can you *really* get one? Or have your parents said no to anything bigger than a hamster? Even if that's the case, you don't have to give up your horsey dreams. You can still learn all about the Morgan horse. Besides, you won't always be a kid. Who knows? Someday you just may have a Morgan horse of your very own!

Chapter One

MEET THE MORGAN HORSE

The Morgan horse is easy to love. It's a high-stepping breed. These horses carry themselves proudly. They hold their heads and tails higher than most horses.

Morgan horses have graceful necks and short, shapely ears. They have broad foreheads and soft, kind eyes. Their manes and tails are long and thick.

How Big Is That Horse?

All horses are measured in hands. One hand is equal to 4 inches (10 centimeters). The Morgan horse is about fourteen hands high at the highest part of its back. The Morgan horse is what's known as a light breed. Light-breed horses weigh less than 1,500 pounds (680 kilograms).

Horsey Math

This equation shows about how high a Morgan horse is in inches and centimeters.

$$
\begin{array}{r}
14 \text{ hands} \\
\times\ 4 \text{ inches (10 cm)} \\
\hline
56 \text{ inches (90 cm)}
\end{array}
$$

A Horse of Many Colors

Morgan horses can be almost any color. Many are brown, black, chestnut (dark reddish brown), or bay (deep red). Some have white markings on their bodies.

A State Symbol in Two States!

The Morgan horse is the state horse of Massachusetts. It's also the state animal of Vermont.

A Joy to Ride

The Morgan horse is gentle and easygoing. It's eager to please its owner. That makes it perfect for children and beginning riders.

Horse Body Basics

You know that horses have a mane, a tail, and four hooves. But can you find a horse's withers? Or its forelock? Let's take a closer look at a horse. Soon you'll be an expert on all the parts that make up these wonderful animals.

back

croup

dock

flank

thigh

tail

hock

barrel

fetlock

poll

mane

forelock

muzzle

withers

cheek

neck

chest

elbow

chestnut

chestnut

cannon

pastern

hoof

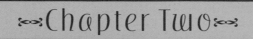

Chapter Two

AN ALL-AMERICAN BREED

The Morgan horse dates back to 1789. That's when a horse named Figure was born in New England. He got his name because he was such a fine figure of a horse.

Yet Figure had more than good looks. He was strong and fast. He could outwork and outrun most horses of the time.

This statue of Figure stands in Vermont.

A New Breed Is Born

In 1791, a schoolteacher named Justin Morgan became Figure's owner. Someone gave Morgan the horse as payment for a debt. Morgan bred Figure with a female horse. Figure's colts and fillies were very much like their father. They were the start of a new breed called the Morgan horse.

As the Nation Grew

Morgan horses were helpful to early settlers heading west. Settlers used the horses in wagon trains (long lines of wagons that settlers used to carry supplies). Miners also relied on Morgan horses. The horses took the miners to California after gold was discovered there in 1848.

An All-Around Horse

Morgan horses soon became very popular. There was little these horses couldn't do. They made great farm horses. They could pull heavy loads. Some became winning racehorses.

Morgan horses were also used a lot during the Civil War (1861–1865). They bravely carried soldiers into battle. They were not shaken by the sights and sounds of fighting.

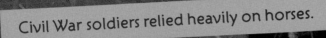

Civil War soldiers relied heavily on horses.

The Pony Express? Oh, Yes!

From 1860 to 1861, Morgan horses were used for a speedy mail service called the pony express. Riders guided their horses in relays over long, rough trails to deliver mail. The horses and riders worked through blizzards as well as under blazing summer sun. The horses had to be strong and fast. Riders knew they could count on Morgan horses to get the job done.

Always a Winner

These days, people still love the Morgan horse. Some use it to pull carriages. It's also great for pleasure riding. These horses do well in the show ring too.

15

Chapter Three

THE REAL DEAL

Would having a Morgan horse really be great? Think before you answer. Owning a horse is much harder than having a hamster. Horse ownership takes a lot of time, work, and money.

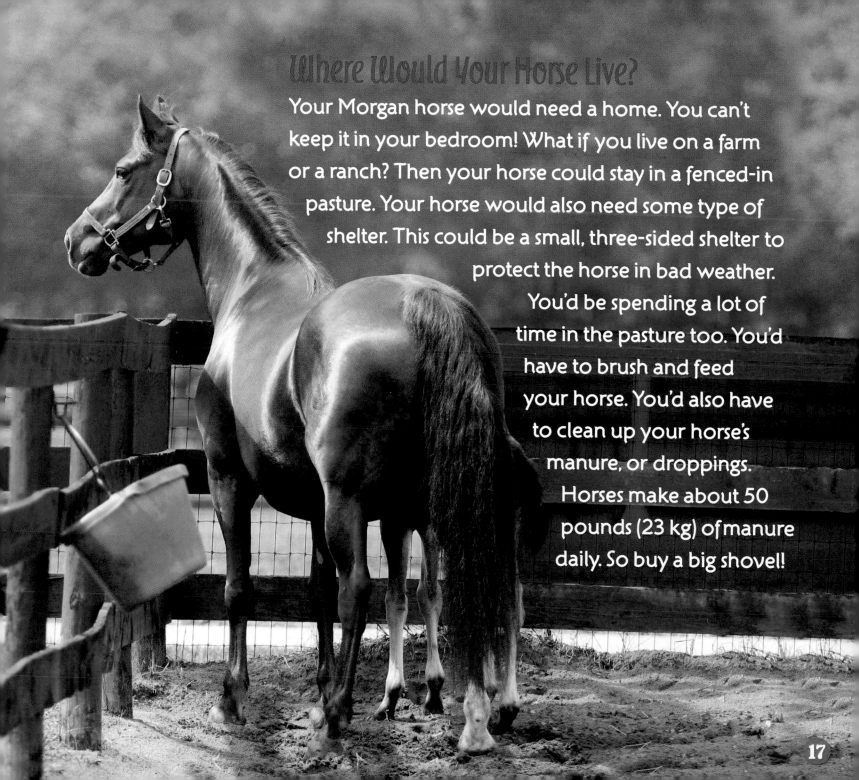

Where Would Your Horse Live?

Your Morgan horse would need a home. You can't keep it in your bedroom! What if you live on a farm or a ranch? Then your horse could stay in a fenced-in pasture. Your horse would also need some type of shelter. This could be a small, three-sided shelter to protect the horse in bad weather. You'd be spending a lot of time in the pasture too. You'd have to brush and feed your horse. You'd also have to clean up your horse's manure, or droppings. Horses make about 50 pounds (23 kg) of manure daily. So buy a big shovel!

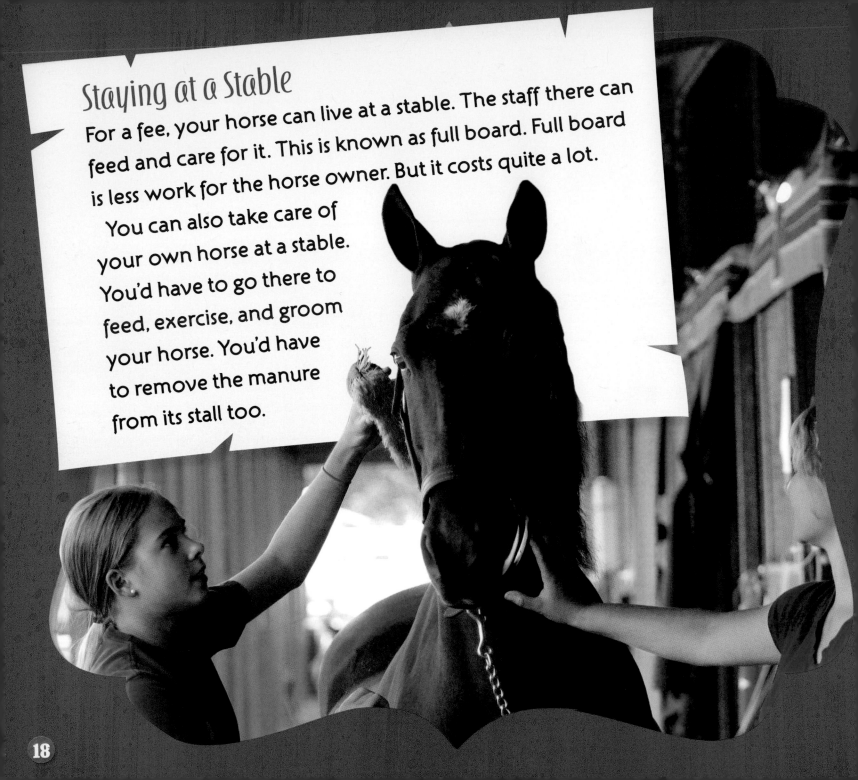

Staying at a Stable

For a fee, your horse can live at a stable. The staff there can feed and care for it. This is known as full board. Full board is less work for the horse owner. But it costs quite a lot. You can also take care of your own horse at a stable. You'd have to go there to feed, exercise, and groom your horse. You'd have to remove the manure from its stall too.

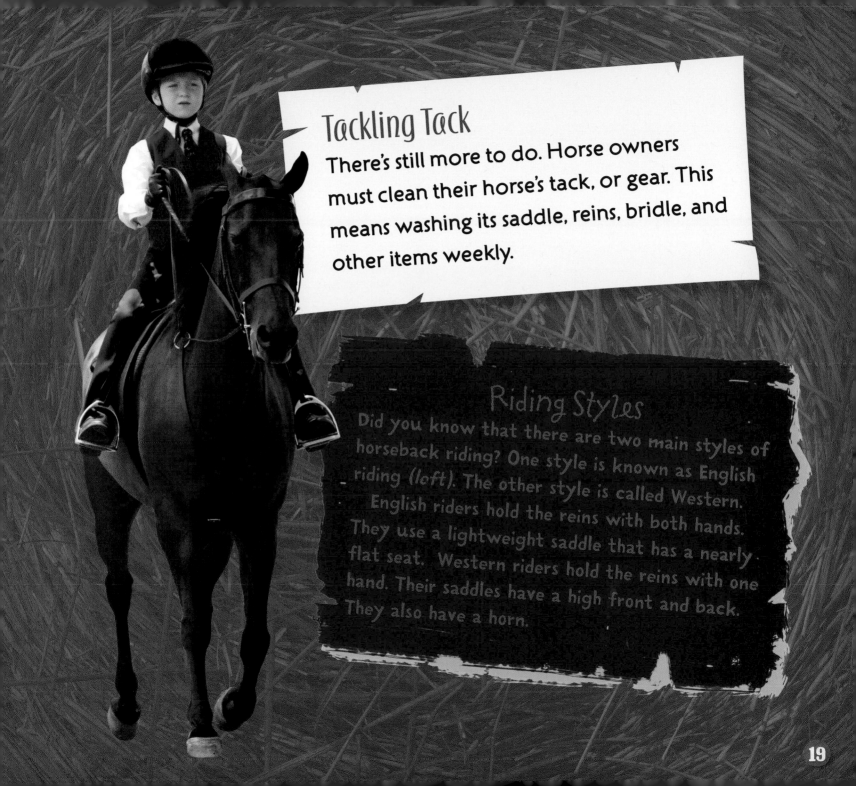

Tackling Tack

There's still more to do. Horse owners must clean their horse's tack, or gear. This means washing its saddle, reins, bridle, and other items weekly.

Riding Styles

Did you know that there are two main styles of horseback riding? One style is known as English riding (left). The other style is called Western. English riders hold the reins with both hands. They use a lightweight saddle that has a nearly flat seat. Western riders hold the reins with one hand. Their saddles have a high front and back. They also have a horn.

19

Moving Along

Horses move in different ways. These are called gaits. Walking is the slowest gait. The horse lifts one foot at a time off the ground. Trotting is a bit faster than walking. The horse moves two of its legs forward at the same time. A canter is faster than a trot. The canter is a three-beat gait. Galloping is the fastest gait of all. A gallop feels like a very fast canter.

Horse Crazy

You don't have to own a horse to enjoy these animals. Here are some other fun things you can do.

Make horses your hobby.
Look for books, magazines, and DVDs on the Morgan horse. Check out any YouTube videos on them. Become an expert on this breed!

Create a Morgan horse scrapbook.
Cut out pictures of Morgan horses. Highlight some prizewinners. Jot down any facts you find about them.

Get up close.
Some summer camps have riding programs. See if you can go to one of these. Or ask your parents if you can take riding lessons. This costs much less than owning a horse.

At some stables, you may be able to get riding lessons for free in exchange for doing chores, such as horse grooming.

Morgan horses are really super. Maybe you'll get to spend some time around them. Or maybe you'll just learn all about this beautiful breed. Either way, you're sure to have fun!

GLOSSARY

bay: deep red

breed: a particular type of horse. Horses of the same breed have the same body shape and general features. *Breed* can also refer to producing horses.

chestnut: dark reddish brown

colt: a young male horse

debt: money owed to someone

filly: a young female horse

full board: an arrangement in which a horse owner pays staff at a stable to feed and care for the horse

gait: a word to describe a horse's movements. The four gaits are walk, trot, canter, and gallop.

groom: to brush and clean a horse

hand: a unit for measuring horses. One hand is equal to 4 inches (10 cm).

horn: a knob at the front of a Western-style saddle

light breed: a term to describe a horse that weighs less than 1,500 pounds (680 kg)

tack: a horse's gear, including its saddle, reins, and bridle

FOR MORE INFORMATION

Brecke, Nicole, and Patricia M. Stockland. *Horses You Can Draw*. Minneapolis: Millbrook Press, 2010. Especially designed for horse lovers, this colorful book shows young readers how to draw different kinds of horses.

Criscione, Rachel Damon. *The Morgan*. New York: PowerKids Press, 2007. Learn more about the Morgan horse in this interesting title.

Horse Fun!
http://www.horsefun.com
This website is all about kids and horses. You'll find lots of horsey quizzes, puzzles, and games here. There are also some handy hints for young riders.

Horse History for Kids
http://www.historyforkids.org/learn/environment/horses.htm
Where did horses come from? When did people first start riding? What did people use horses for? Learn the answer to these and other questions at this interesting website.

McDaniel, Lurlene. *A Horse for Mandy*. Minneapolis: Darby Creek, 2004. On her thirteenth birthday, Mandy gets her dream gift—a horse of her own. But will Mandy and her horse be able to save her best friend when tragedy strikes?

Nelson, Robin. *From Foal to Horse*. Minneapolis: Lerner Publications Company, 2012. Learn how a foal grows to adulthood in this fun book.

LERNER SOURCE
Expand learning beyond the printed book. Download free, complementary educational resources for this book from our website, www.lernerresource.com.

INDEX